KING'S HORSES AND MEN

Keith Bethard

ISBN-13: 9781234567890
ISBN-10: 1477123456

Cover design by: Art Painter
Library of Congress Control Number: 2018675309
Printed in the United States of America

Reborn from ashes
From spiders' corpses I rise
Webs spun of deceit

KEITH BETHARD

Drowning in cement
Hand outstretched toward the sky
Someone give me air

Ruby encrusted
Silver knife ripples in me
Transmission throughout

California
American flags waving
Breathing burns my lungs

Harps know only love
Violins play in times of war
Constant orchestra

Spirits of foxes
Elegantly perched on trees
Weaving fate through steps

Flowing soft flight paths
River water in wood bowls
White diamonds to drink

KEITH BETHARD

Become gods, too strong
To care about your best friend
Who does not love me

Waves pull me under
Sinking into the abyss
Breathing salt water

Morning dew at dawn
Hummingbirds drink the sunrise
I can find hope here

Sweet baby Jane runs
With scissors like the Eiffel
Does not yet fear death

KEITH BETHARD

Hades packs my heart
For lunch at the graveyard shift
He likes the sour taste

A bird in my hands
So fragile And tender…
I control your life.

Make strings from my tears
Tapestries by Athena
Beauty is money

Rip myself open
Watercolor images
I will become art

KEITH BETHARD

Bombs are deafening
American symphony
But is this the dream

Facts about myself
Serpents whisper while I sleep
Turn me into eve

Evening in Britain
Orange acrylic sky Now
The sun sets on you

I bring down the sky
Crushing all who have hurt me
My world is at peace

Dreams of gasoline
I hate you. Truly, Deeply!
I'm on fire again

Briar rose in slumber
I do wish death upon you
Prolonging beauty

Arms made from the clouds
My total divinity
Rain and sun controlled

Dandelion petals
Throw themselves from the body
To escape your evil

25

Vines grow on the walls
Of my Victorian manor
Where I go to weep

KEITH BETHARD

Sometimes I think that
The birds are my old, dead friends
Begging me to run

Giving myself cuts
On the pages while I write
Like finger painting

KEITH BETHARD

Quill against the sword
Has no merit to the man
Who points here the gun

Butterfly in rain
From hubris shall death befall
May she fall gently

Had Adam and Eve
rebuked, Cast out the serpent
Would I be happy?

I keep water close
A chaser for thoughts of you
To cleanse my body

I miss the feeling
Accomplishment in starving
Was empty, felt whole.

Painting four walls the
Color of my lover's eyes
Tearing down four walls

My minefield mind
Impossible to traverse
Without casualty

Bare your fangs at me
The white winter wolf in snow
To love is to die

KEITH BETHARD

Father of Eden
In my bloodstream flowers bloom
Livestreams soft on TV

My heart is fools gold
Structurally different
My nature is dark

KEITH BETHARD

Wooden fans break in
Favor of cherry lip gloss
Shifting traditions

Graceful heron proud
Finding herself in lake views
Where she lays to hunt

40

She puts me to bed
Soft mother sings me requiems
The evening bells toll

God does not love me
I take care of things I love
He tries to kill me

Three years overwhelmed
By television static
Chained under waves

uncharted waters
i can't make it on my own
navigate for me

KEITH BETHARD

My blood on the rocks
Oceanic lemon water
Life on the top shelf

Hollywood's dead now.
Up in flames. A false idol.
A reflection past

Molasses floods from
Cotton candy thunderclouds
Sweetened disaster

On taste, I ponder.
Does my opinion matter
If they don't listen?

Morning ocean view
Beautiful, untouchable,
I am Atlantis.

I'm like fine china
Across the floor I shatter
King's horses and men.

I have been writing
My own eulogy for years
Publishing it, too.

KEITH BETHARD

I'm only a fan
Of summer because of you
And how you loathe it

The balcony calls
For me to leap, create paints
Self tortured artist

Foxes with nine tails
Guide me through forests in dreams
Unseen intention

dances in streets at night
Street lights blurred by welling tears
Spotlight of the moon

Pink Himalayan salt
Makes mountains around the lake
My thoughts pour out of

Unlike snow I thaw
Into ice. Hold myself still.
Frigid under the sun.

Patent leather black
Trees hang their lace orange fruit
In my dominion

Genesis painting
Oil on canvas like the greats
Ultramarine sky

Automaton hearts
Gears turning and blood churning
Man-made emotion

Vineyards in clouds
Grape juice runs, stain purple streaks
Organic sunset

KEITH BETHARD

Modern alchemy
Ones and zeroes into gold
new transmutation

Acidic living
Things touched begin to melt
Midas in citrus

Japanese breakfast
Susanoo finds himself in
Tea leaf hurricanes

Hot summer days, long

car rides beckoned off high cliffs

Now this is living

KEITH BETHARD

Wood woven baskets

Hand-picked strawberries inlaid

My peaches ruined

calydonian hunt

rebellious retribution

Artemis strikes me

KEITH BETHARD

My Georgia peaches

grown by someone I once loved

crushed under my foot.

Babylon gardens

hanging off the horizon

built in your image

alabama girls

play house in the yard while dad

prays to have a son